Documents for Democracy

Building America and Literacy Skills Through Primary Sources

Volume 3: 20th Century

Prepared by
Veronica Burchard
Illustrations by Nicole M. Blank

*Dedicated to my loving husband,
Kyle Burchard,
as well as my mentor and friend,
Claire McCaffery Griffin*

Unless otherwise noted, no part of this publication may be reproduced, stored, sourced off for use in other publications, or transmitted, in any form or by any means, electronic, mechanical, photocopying, recording or otherwise, without the prior written permission of the American Institute for History Education.

Edited by Matthew F. Galella
Design and typography by KJD Communications

Copyright © 2010 American Institute for History Education
All rights reserved

ISBN-13: 978-0-9826244-2-5

Printed in the United States of America
July 2010

Visit **www.aihe-bookstore.com**

Table of Contents

Theodore Roosevelt's Speech at the Minnesota State Fair 3

Carrie Chapman Catt's Address to Congress 15

Malcolm X's OAAU Founding Rally Address 27

President Reagan's Challenger Disaster Address 39

About the Author 50

Introduction

It was September 2, 1901. The 20th century had just begun. The vice president of the United States gazed at the happy crowd that had gathered at the Minnesota State Fair. Over the sounds of the livestock and children laughing, he began his speech.

Theodore Roosevelt

Theodore Roosevelt expressed his excitement and pride in America. Roosevelt believed the bold and strong spirit of America's pioneers would help America succeed in the new century. He saw chances for America to be powerful in the world.

He also spoke about an African proverb that meant a lot to him: "Speak softly and carry a big stick — you will go far." Roosevelt explained what the words meant to him. He believed people should say what they mean, and mean what they say. Nations, too, should be respectful to each other, but always be prepared to back up words with action.

Less than two weeks later, President William McKinley was assassinated, and Theodore Roosevelt became president. His "big stick" approach to other nations helped to grow America's navy, and America became more involved in world affairs in the 20th century.

What Is a Primary Source?

A primary source is a piece of history. It is an artifact from a time period, like a diary, a speech, a newspaper article, or a photograph. In this chapter, you will study *Theodore Roosevelt's Speech at the Minnesota State Fair* as a primary source from 1901, as a way to learn about that time period of American history.

Activating Prior Knowledge: Questions for Pre-Reading Discussion

1. What do you know about President Theodore Roosevelt? What do you associate with him?
2. Have you ever seen a picture of Mount Rushmore?
3. What do you know about the start of the 20th century?
4. How do you think people felt at the beginning of the new century?
5. How do you think your parents felt in the year 2001?
6. Have you heard the phrase "Speak softly and carry a big stick"? What do you think it means?

Vocabulary and Context Questions

Complete this page as you read. Using context clues and/or a dictionary, define each word:

Vocabulary

pioneers:

expansive:

privilege:

acquainted:

blusters:

civility:

avail:

evident:

tolerate:

moderate:

attainment:

prime:

Context Questions

1. Who delivered this speech?
2. When did he deliver it?
3. What was his purpose?
4. Who listened to this speech?

We are a nation of pioneers and therefore our nation has in it more energy,
more expansive power than any other in the wide world.

To us is given the privilege of playing a leading part in the century that has just opened.

A good many of you are probably acquainted with the old proverb: "Speak softly and carry a big stick — you will go far."

If a man continually blusters, if he lacks civility,
a big stick will not save him from trouble;
and neither will speaking softly avail,
if back of the softness there does not lie strength, power.

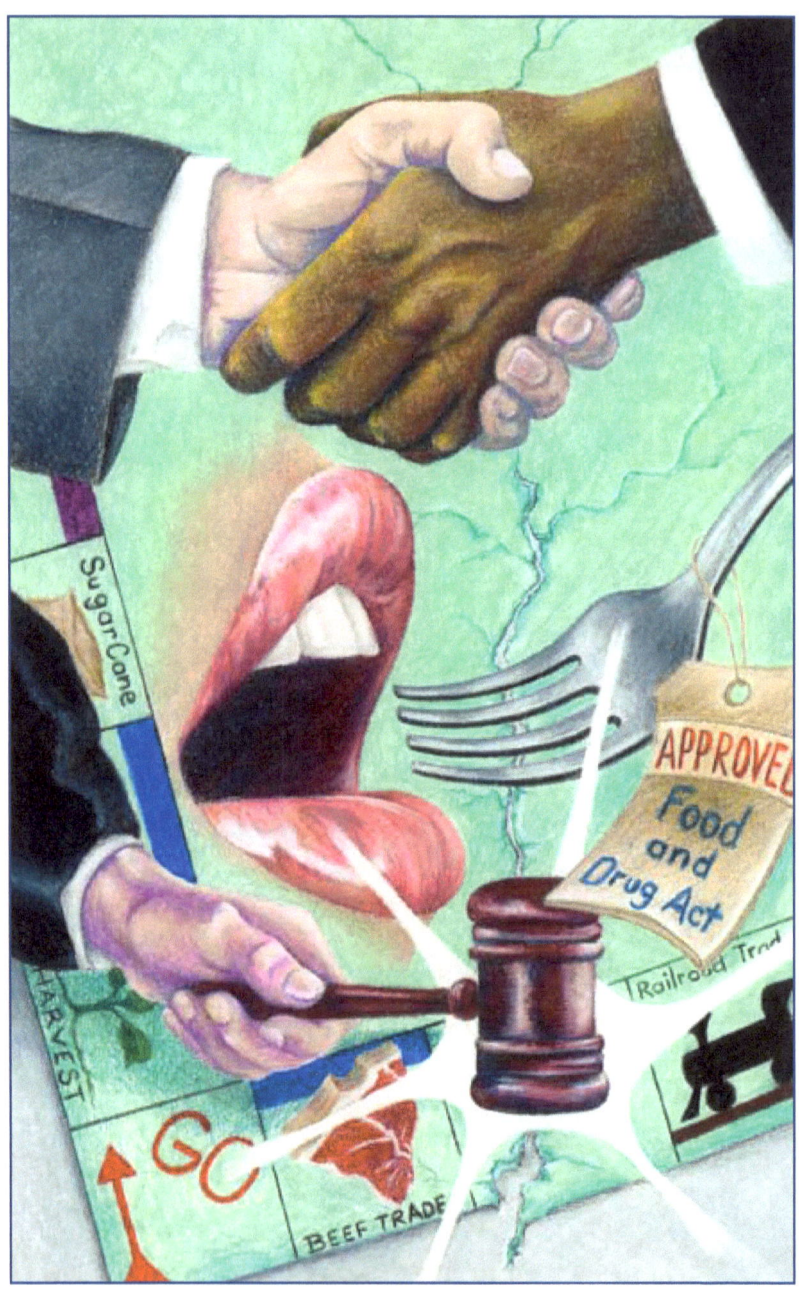

Let us make it evident that we intend to do justice. Then let us make it equally evident that we will not tolerate injustice being done to us in return.

We use no words which we are not prepared to back up with deeds, and while our speech is always moderate, we are ready and willing to make it good.

Such an attitude will be the surest possible guarantee of that self-respecting peace, the attainment of which is and must ever be the prime aim of a self-governing people.

Theodore Roosevelt's Speech at the Minnesota State Fair

We are a nation of pioneers and therefore our nation has in it more energy, more expansive power than any other in the wide world.

To us is given the privilege of playing a leading part in the century that has just opened.

A good many of you are probably acquainted with the old proverb: "Speak softly and carry a big stick — you will go far."

If a man continually blusters, if he lacks civility, a big stick will not save him from trouble; and neither will speaking softly avail, if back of the softness there does not lie strength, power.

Let us make it evident that we intend to do justice. Then let us make it equally evident that we will not tolerate injustice being done to us in return.

Let us further make it evident that we use no words which we are not prepared to back up with deeds, and that while our speech is always moderate, we are ready and willing to make it good.

Such an attitude will be the surest possible guarantee of that self-respecting peace, the attainment of which is and must ever be the prime aim of a self-governing people.

Introduction

The Constitution did not protect a woman's right to vote when it was first written. Only white men had this right. The Fifteenth Amendment gave black men the right to vote, but as of 1917, women still did not have a say in choosing America's leaders or what kinds of laws were passed. The United States was based on the people governing themselves. But women had no voice in government.

Carrie Chapman Catt

Beginning in the mid 1800s, women across America had been talking with each other, having meetings, and forming groups to try to win the vote for female citizens of the United States. One of these groups was called the National American Woman Suffrage Association (NAWSA). Carrie Chapman Catt was the president of NAWSA.

By the end of the 1800s, some states had given women the right to vote. But Catt believed that for women to be able to vote everywhere, an amendment to the federal Constitution was needed. She went before Congress in 1917 and gave an important speech. She asked the senators and representatives from all the states to make a choice. Would they support votes for women, or work against them?

What Is a Primary Source?

A primary source is a piece of history. It is an artifact from a time period, like a diary, a speech, a newspaper article, or a photograph. In this chapter, you will study the speech *Carrie Chapman Catt's Address to Congress* as a primary source from 1917, as a way to learn about that time period of American history.

Activating Prior Knowledge: Questions for Pre-Reading Discussion

1. Did you know that American women did not have the right to vote until the Nineteenth Amendment was adopted in 1920?
2. Have you ever heard of women's suffragists? What do you know about them?
3. Why is voting important in the United States?
4. Why do you think women wanted the right to vote?
5. What kinds of things do you think Carrie Chapman Catt said to members of Congress (who were all men except for one congresswoman) about votes for women?

Vocabulary and Context Questions

Complete this page as you read. Using context clues and/or a dictionary, define each word:

Vocabulary

suffrage:

inevitable:

distinct:

revolution:

rebellion:

deny:

compel:

enfranchisement:

pledged:

hinder:

Context Questions

1. Who delivered this speech?
2. When did she deliver it?
3. What was her purpose?
4. Who listened to this speech?

Woman suffrage is inevitable.
Three distinct causes made it inevitable.

First, the history of our country.
Ours is a nation born of revolution, of rebellion.

Second, the suffrage for women already established in the United States makes women suffrage for the nation inevitable. No one will deny it. The only question left is when and how will it be completely established.

Third, the leadership of the United States in world democracy compels the enfranchisement of its own women.

Your party platforms have pledged women suffrage. Then why not be honest, why not put the amendment through Congress? We shall have a happier nation, we women will be free to support loyally the party of our choice, and we shall be far prouder of our history.

The time for woman suffrage has come.
The woman's hour has struck.

Holding her torch aloft, liberty is pointing the way onward and upward and saying to America, "Come." Woman suffrage is coming — you know it. Will you help or hinder it?

Carrie Chapman Catt's Address to Congress

Woman suffrage is inevitable.
Three distinct causes made it inevitable.

First, the history of our country. Ours is a nation born of revolution, of rebellion.

Second, the suffrage for women already established in the United States makes women suffrage for the nation inevitable. No one will deny it. The only question left is when and how will it be completely established.

Third, the leadership of the United States in world democracy compels the enfranchisement of its own women.

Your party platforms have pledged women suffrage. Then why not be honest, why not put the amendment through Congress?

We shall have a happier nation, we women will be free to support loyally the party of our choice, and we shall be far prouder of our history.

The time for woman suffrage has come.
The woman's hour has struck.

Holding her torch aloft, liberty is pointing the way onward and upward and saying to America, "Come." Woman suffrage is coming — you know it. Will you help or hinder it?

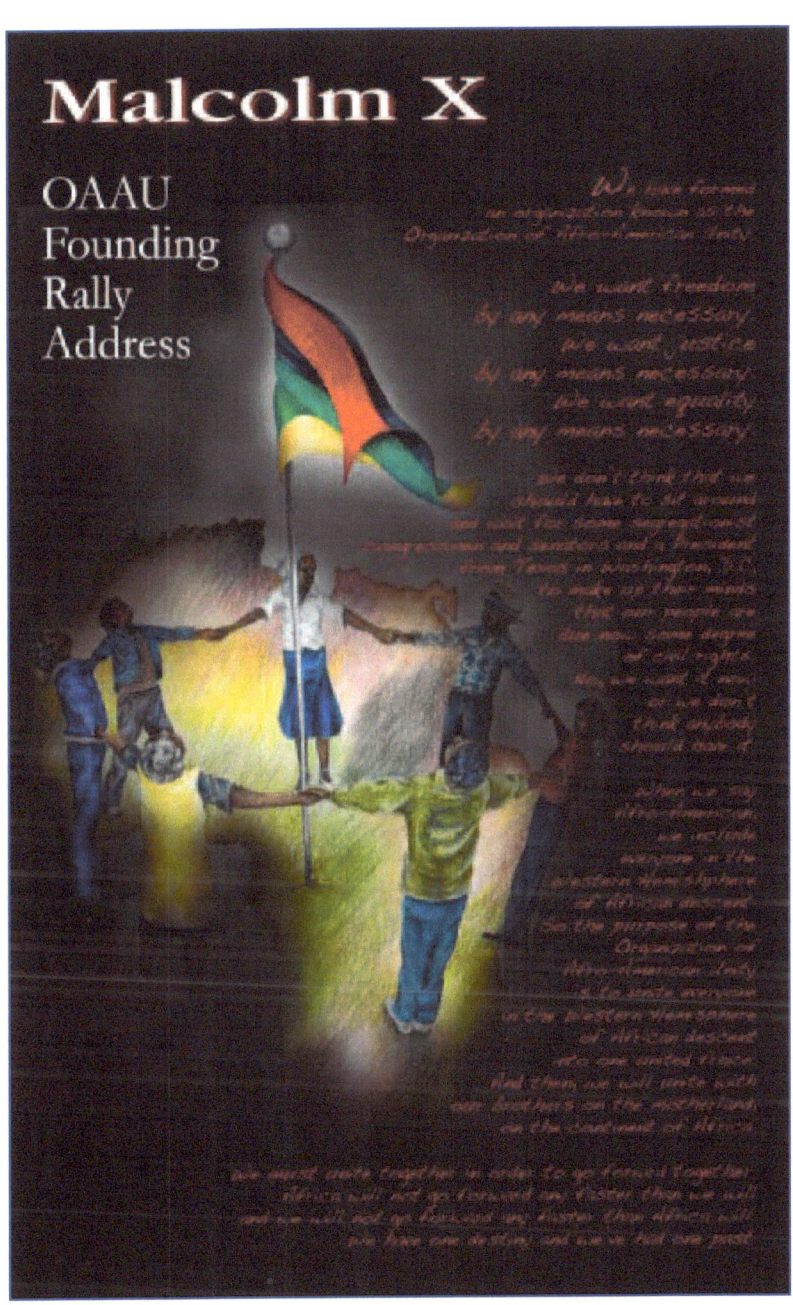

Introduction

The Civil War ended in 1865. The Constitution was amended to say the government must treat all people equally under the law. Even so, African Americans faced discrimination after the Civil War through to the 20th century.

Malcolm X

Famous civil rights leaders like Martin Luther King Jr. preached nonviolent protest as a way of fighting racism. Civil rights leader Malcolm X saw things differently. Malcolm X believed that nonviolence would not win over violent racism. He believed African Americans should unite and fight back against racist whites. He even thought African Americans should separate from whites and form their own independent communities.

Malcolm X had once belonged to the Nation of Islam. He left the Nation of Islam so he could work to unite all people of African descent, of all religions. He helped form the Organization of Afro-American Unity, or OAAU. He spoke at its founding rally in 1964. He talked about his belief that African Americans shared the same destiny as their brothers and sisters in Africa.

What Is a Primary Source?

A primary source is a piece of history. It is an artifact from a time period, like a diary, a speech, a newspaper article, or a photograph. In this chapter, you will study *Malcolm X's OAAU Founding Rally Address* as a primary source from 1964, as a way to learn about that time period of American history.

Activating Prior Knowledge: Questions for Pre-Reading Discussion

1. Have you ever heard of the Civil Rights Movement? When did it take place? What do you know about it?
2. Have you ever heard the names Martin Luther King Jr., Rosa Parks, or Malcolm X? Who were they?
3. Do you know what the word "segregation" means?
4. If you were asked to describe a perfect America in three words, what words would you use?
5. Have you heard the phrase "The ends justify the means"? What do you think it means?
6. Do you belong to any clubs at school? Do you play on a team, or belong to any other organizations outside of school like 4-H, or Boy Scouts or Girl Scouts?
7. Why do people like to form and join clubs?

Vocabulary and Context Questions

Complete the pages as you read. Using context clues and/or a dictionary, define each word:

Vocabulary

unity:

means:

justice:

equality:

segregationist:

descent:

destiny:

Context Questions

1. Who delivered this speech?
2. When did he deliver it?
3. What was his purpose?
4. Who listened to this speech?

We have formed an organization known as the Organization of Afro-American Unity.

We want freedom by any means necessary.

We want justice by any means necessary.
We want equality by any means necessary.

We don't think that we should have to sit around and wait for some segregationist congressmen and senators and a President from Texas in Washington, D.C., to make up their minds that our people are due now civil rights. No, we want it now or we don't think anybody should have it.

So the purpose of the Organization of Afro-American Unity is to unite everyone in the Western Hemisphere of African descent into one united force. And then, we will unite with our brothers on the motherland, on the continent of Africa.

We must unite together in order to go forward together.

Africa will not go forward any faster than we will and we will not go forward any faster than Africa will. We have one destiny and we've had one past.

Malcolm X's OAAU Founding Rally Address

We have formed an organization known as the Organization of Afro-American Unity.

We want freedom by any means necessary.
We want justice by any means necessary.
We want equality by any means necessary.

We don't think that we should have to sit around and wait for some segregationist congressmen and senators and a President from Texas in Washington, D.C., to make up their minds that our people are due now some degree of civil rights.

No, we want it now or we don't think anybody should have it.

When we say Afro-American, we include everyone in the Western Hemisphere of African descent.

So the purpose of the Organization of Afro-American Unity is to unite everyone in the Western Hemisphere of African descent into one united force. And then, we will unite with our brothers on the motherland, on the continent of Africa.

We must unite together in order to go forward together. Africa will not go forward any faster than we will and we will not go forward any faster than Africa will.
We have one destiny and we've had one past.

Introduction

Late in the morning on January 28, 1986, the space shuttle Challenger lifted off from Kennedy Space Center in Florida. It was a very special event because a schoolteacher was part of the crew and would be going into space. The event was televised and people everywhere — including schoolchildren in classrooms across the country — were watching.

Ronald Reagan

Just more than a minute into its flight, something terrible happened. The shuttle broke apart in a cloud of smoke. People everywhere were shocked and saddened.

President Ronald Reagan had been planning to give his yearly State of the Union address that night. But he decided it was more important to talk to his fellow citizens about the Challenger disaster. President Reagan gave a speech that evening in which he expressed his sorrow for the loss of the seven brave people aboard the Challenger. He also praised the daring and heroic ways they had lived their lives.

What Is a Primary Source?

A primary source is a piece of history. It is an artifact from a time period, like a diary, a speech, a newspaper article, or a photograph. In this chapter, you will study *President Reagan's Challenger Disaster Address* as a primary source from 1986, as a way to learn about that time period of American history.

Activating Prior Knowledge: Questions for Pre-Reading Discussion

1. Have you ever watched the space shuttle take off or land?
2. Have you watched news reports about the International Space Station?
3. What do you know about the Challenger shuttle disaster?
4. Why do you think President Reagan decided to make a speech to the country on the day of the Challenger disaster?
5. The name of the shuttle that exploded was the Challenger. What does that word make you think of?
6. What challenges have you faced in your own life? What challenges does your class take on? Your city? Your country?

Vocabulary and Context Questions

Complete the pages as you read. Using context clues and/or a dictionary, define each word:

Vocabulary

challenge:

mourning:

tragedy:

wonders:

pioneer:

surly:

bonds:

Context Questions

1. Who delivered this speech?
2. When was it written?
3. What was its purpose?
4. Who listened to this speech?

Today is a day for mourning and remembering.
Nancy and I are pained to the core by the tragedy of the shuttle Challenger.
We know we share this pain with all of the people of our country.

This is truly a national loss.

We've grown used to wonders in this century. It's hard to dazzle us. But for twenty-five years the United States space program has been doing just that. We've grown used to the idea of space, and perhaps we forget that we've only just begun.

We're still pioneers.
They, the members of the Challenger crew, were pioneers.

The future doesn't belong to the fainthearted;
it belongs to the brave.

The crew of the space shuttle Challenger
honored us by the manner
in which they lived their lives.

We will never forget them,
nor the last time we saw them, this morning,
as they prepared for the journey and waved goodbye
and "slipped the surly bonds of earth" to "touch the
face of God."

President Reagan's Challenger Disaster Address

Today is a day for mourning and remembering.

Nancy and I are pained to the core by the tragedy of the shuttle Challenger.

We know we share this pain with all of the people of our country.

This is truly a national loss.

We've grown used to wonders in this century. It's hard to dazzle us.

But for twenty-five years the United States space program has been doing just that.

We've grown used to the idea of space, and perhaps we forget that we've only just begun.

We're still pioneers. They, the members of the Challenger crew, were pioneers.

The future doesn't belong to the fainthearted; it belongs to the brave.

The crew of the space shuttle Challenger honored us by the manner in which they lived their lives.

We will never forget them, nor the last time we saw them, this morning, as they prepared for the journey and waved goodbye and "slipped the surly bonds of earth" to "touch the face of God."

About the Author

After teaching for seven years, Veronica Burchard became the Director of Curriculum Development for an educational nonprofit organization near Washington, D.C. She earned her bachelor's and master's degrees in English from the University of Florida, and her interests include American literature and civic education. Veronica lives with her husband, two sons and a very hungry guinea pig in Fairfax, Virginia.

www.ingramcontent.com/pod-product-compliance
Lightning Source LLC
Chambersburg PA
CBHW041526090426
42736CB00035B/24